D1032412

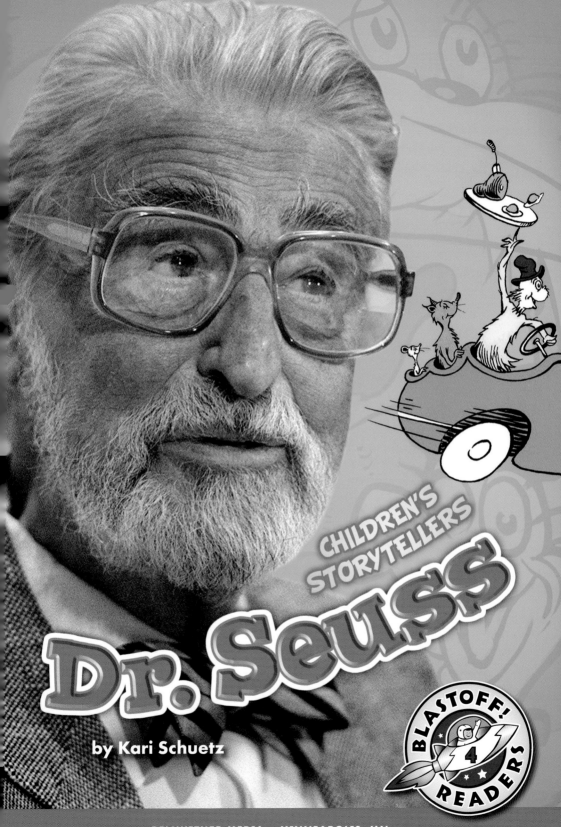

CHILDREN'S STORYTELLERS

Dr. Seuss

by Kari Schuetz

BLASTOFF! READERS

4

BELLWETHER MEDIA • MINNEAPOLIS, MN

Note to Librarians, Teachers, and Parents:

Blastoff! Readers are carefully developed by literacy experts and combine standards-based content with developmentally appropriate text.

Level 1 provides the most support through repetition of high-frequency words, light text, predictable sentence patterns, and strong visual support.

Level 2 offers early readers a bit more challenge through varied simple sentences, increased text load, and less repetition of high-frequency words.

Level 3 advances early-fluent readers toward fluency through increased text and concept load, less reliance on visuals, longer sentences, and more literary language.

Level 4 builds reading stamina by providing more text per page, increased use of punctuation, greater variation in sentence patterns, and increasingly challenging vocabulary.

Level 5 encourages children to move from "learning to read" to "reading to learn" by providing even more text, varied writing styles, and less familiar topics.

Whichever book is right for your reader, Blastoff! Readers are the perfect books to build confidence and encourage a love of reading that will last a lifetime!

This edition first published in 2016 by Bellwether Media, Inc.

No part of this publication may be reproduced in whole or in part without written permission of the publisher. For information regarding permission, write to Bellwether Media, Inc., Attention: Permissions Department, 5357 Penn Avenue South, Minneapolis, MN 55419.

Library of Congress Cataloging-in-Publication Data

Schuetz, Kari.
    Dr. Seuss / by Kari Schuetz.
       pages cm. – (Blastoff! Readers: Children's Storytellers)
    Summary: "Simple text and full-color photography introduce readers to Dr. Seuss. Developed by literacy experts for students in kindergarten through third grade"– Provided by publisher.
    Includes bibliographical references and index.
    Audience: Ages 5-8
    Audience: K to grade 3
    ISBN 978-1-62617-265-4 (hardcover: alk. paper)
    1. Seuss, Dr.–Juvenile literature. 2. Authors, American–20th century–Biography–Juvenile literature. 3. Illustrators–United States–Biography–Juvenile literature. 4. Children's stories–Authorship–Juvenile literature. I. Title.
PS3513.E2Z84 2016
813'.52–dc23
    [B]
                                                    2015012552

Text copyright © 2016 by Bellwether Media, Inc. BLASTOFF! READERS and associated logos are trademarks and/or registered trademarks of Bellwether Media, Inc. SCHOLASTIC, CHILDREN'S PRESS, and associated logos are trademarks and/or registered trademarks of Scholastic Inc.

Printed in the United States of America, North Mankato, MN.

Table of Contents

Who Was Dr. Seuss?

Dr. Seuss was a master storyteller. The man made mischief with a cat in a hat. He also created an imaginary town called Whoville.

"I like nonsense, it wakes up the brain cells."
Dr. Seuss

fun fact

Seuss is supposed to rhyme with *voice*, not *goose*. The doctor never minded that people mispronounced it.

For more than 50 years, the doctor created strange characters and charming rhymes to make reading fun.

Dr. Seuss was born Theodor "Ted" Seuss Geisel on March 2, 1904. He grew up in Springfield, Massachusetts. His family ran a successful business there.

"**Words and pictures [are] yin and yang.**"
Dr. Seuss

Springfield, Massachusetts

N

W   E

S

fun fact
One of Ted's favorite comics was
Krazy Kat. The cat in the strip led
Ted to create his own cat character.

As a boy, Ted enjoyed reading books and
comics. His mom's bedtime rhymes made
him want to write funny poems. He also
drew a lot. Many sketches were of animals
at the local zoo.

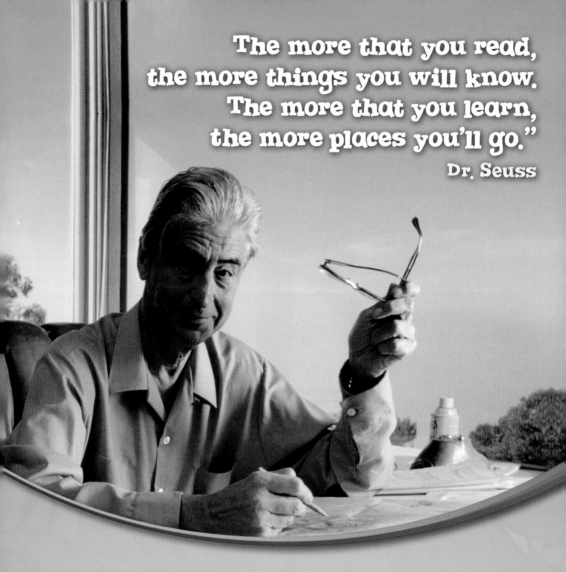

"The more that you read,
the more things you will know.
The more that you learn,
the more places you'll go."

Dr. Seuss

After high school, Ted left for college.
He studied English at Dartmouth College
in New Hampshire. He became head
editor of the school's magazine, the
Jack-O-Lantern. This is when he first
used his famous **pen name**, Seuss.

Then Ted studied at Oxford University in England to become a professor. However, he soon stopped to focus on his art.

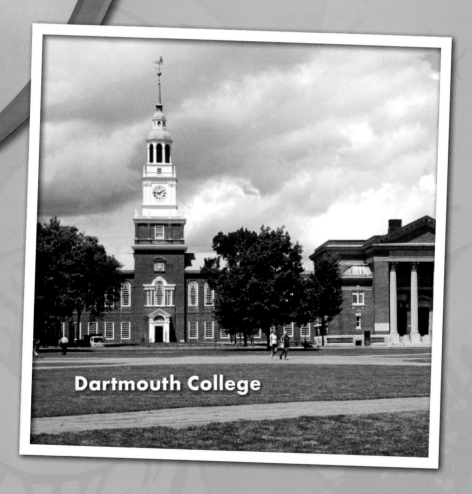

Dartmouth College

Cartoonist and Ad Man

Ted moved to New York City to find a job.
He drew cartoons for *Judge* magazine.
Then he started to create **advertisements**.
His most popular ones were for Flit
bug spray.

fun fact

The Saturday Evening Post was the first big-time magazine to print one of Ted's cartoons.

During World War II, Ted drew more than 400 **political cartoons**. He also made films and other training materials for the United States Army.

A Published Author

Ted was under a **contract** for his advertising work. The agreement limited his other creative projects. Still, he had the freedom to **publish** for children.

Unfortunately, editors **rejected** his book ideas over and over. Finally, *And to Think That I Saw It on Mulberry Street* was printed. It had taken more than 20 failed tries for this to happen!

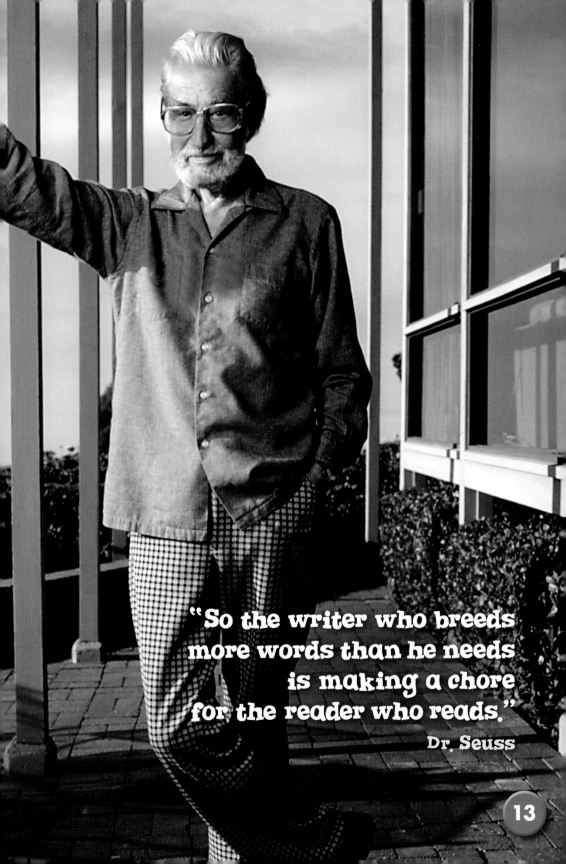

"So the writer who breeds
more words than he needs
is making a chore
for the reader who reads."

Dr. Seuss

In the 1950s, the United States had many struggling young readers. Some people blamed boring books. To respond, two publishers asked Ted to create a fun, easy read.

Ted pulled words from a list for beginning readers. He used the 236 chosen words to write *The Cat in the Hat*. Kids and adults both praised the finished book.

fun fact

A few years later, Ted wrote *Green Eggs and Ham* with only 50 words!

Ted's silly approach to writing attracted readers. He organized simple words into clever rhymes. He even made up new words, such as *nerd*.

SELECTED WORKS

And to Think That I Saw It on Mulberry Street (1937)

The 500 Hats of Bartholomew Cubbins (1938)

McElligot's Pool (1947)

Bartholomew and the Oobleck (1949)

If I Ran the Zoo (1950)

Horton Hears a Who! (1954)

The Cat in the Hat (1957)

How the Grinch Stole Christmas! (1957)

Green Eggs and Ham (1960)

One Fish Two Fish Red Fish Blue Fish (1960)

The Lorax (1971)

Oh, the Places You'll Go! (1990)

By **Dr. Seuss**

One fish

two fish

red fish

blue fish

"I think I could draw normally if I wanted to, but I see no reason to re-create something that's already created." Dr. Seuss

Playful illustrations support his text and offer bonus details. They let readers see the grumpy Grinch, the happy Whos, and other interesting characters. Strong outlines, **motion lines**, and bright colors help everything pop off the page.

Ted received a special Pulitzer Prize in 1984 for his effect on reading.

Ted did not pack his books with text. Still, he found ways to say a lot with his words. Common **themes** include being good to others and yourself.

Some of Ted's stories share his beliefs. He showed in *Yertle the Turtle* how a **dictator** is a villain. With *The Lorax*, he urged readers to care more about nature.

POP CULTURE CONNECTION

The book *How the Grinch Stole Christmas!* has been adapted into many forms. The story hit television in 1966, the stage in 1994, and movie theaters in 2000.

THE GRINCH

Ted passed away in 1991. However, his **classics** are here to stay. The books have a magic about them. They turn young children into book lovers. They push all readers to stand up for their beliefs.

WHAT PET SHOULD I GET?

By Dr. Seuss

fun fact

What Pet Should I Get? was first published in 2015. Ted's wife discovered the work after his death.

IMPORTANT DATES

1904: Theodor "Ted" Seuss Geisel is born on March 2.

1925: Ted first uses Seuss as his pen name.

1928: Ted begins creating advertisements for Flit bug spray.

1937: Ted's first children's book, *And to Think That I Saw It on Mulberry Street,* is published.

1948: *McElligot's Pool* is the first of three books to earn Caldecott Honors for its artwork.

1957: *The Cat in the Hat* is published for beginning readers.

1984: Ted wins a special Pulitzer Prize.

1991: Ted passes away on September 24.

2000: *Seussical,* a musical, comes to the stage.

2000: *How the Grinch Stole Christmas!* is Ted's first book to become a movie.

2004: Ted is awarded a star on the Hollywood Walk of Fame.

2015: *What Pet Should I Get?* is published.

For years to come, fans will celebrate Dr. Seuss Day on March 2!

Glossary

advertisements—visuals that make people aware of products and programs

classics—works that will remain popular for a long time because of their excellence

comics—cartoons that tell stories

contract—an official written agreement of terms

dictator—a leader who rules with complete control and often uses his or her power in harmful ways

motion lines—lines that appear close to a character or object to illustrate movement

pen name—a name used by a writer instead of the writer's real name

political cartoons—cartoons that comment on the government or current events

publish—to print someone's work for a public audience

rejected—turned down

themes—important ideas or messages

To Learn More

AT THE LIBRARY

Foran, Jill. *Dr. Seuss*. New York, N.Y.: AV2 by Weigl, 2013.

Krull, Kathleen. *The Boy on Fairfield Street: How Ted Geisel Grew Up to Become Dr. Seuss*. New York, N.Y.: Random House, 2004.

Seuss, Dr. *Oh, the Places You'll Go!* New York, N.Y.: Random House, 1990.

ON THE WEB

Learning more about Dr. Seuss is as easy as 1, 2, 3.

1. Go to www.factsurfer.com.

2. Enter "Dr. Seuss" into the search box.

3. Click the "Surf" button and you will see a list of related web sites.

With factsurfer.com, finding more information is just a click away.

Index

The images in this book are reproduced through the courtesy of: Associated Press, front cover, p. 20 (left); Dr. Seuss Estate/ Splash News/ Corbis, front cover (illustration), p. 17; Ron Ellis, front cover (background), all interior backgrounds; William James Warren/ Science Faction/ Corbis, p. 4; Wisconsinart, p. 5; Library of Congress, p. 6; Old Paper Studios/ Alamy, p. 7; James L. Amos/ Corbis, p. 8; BRT Photo/ Alamy, p. 9; Bettman/ Corbis, p. 10; mooziic/ Alamy, p. 11; Bellwether Media, p. 12; Aaron Rapoport/ Corbis, pp. 12-13; Julie Clopper, pp. 14, 15, 16; Mark Kauffman/ Getty Images, p. 18; AF Archive/ Alamy, p. 19; PR Newswire/ Associated Press, p. 20 (right); Joshua Daniels, p. 21.